JEWELS OF THE GAME

How to Get a Job Working in Sports ©

JEWELS OF THE GAME

How to Get a Job Working in Sports ©

Ancel R. Pratt III

Edited by Lorrie-Ann Diaz and Keonna Pratt

ISBN 978-0-557-76910-0

Introduction

My intention for putting this book together is to give you a crash course on how to get a job working in sports. Of course, this doesn't cover all aspects of the sports industry, but it will definitely give you a strong foundation on how to get in, and provide insight on the common mistakes many people make.

I wasn't as fortunate as you are to have this blueprint to follow. I sincerely hope this helps you to reach your goals. In return, there may come a time when you have the ability to share some encouraging words to help some youth with reaching their goals. I hope you pay it forward.

Dedication

First I would like to thank the Most High for making me who I am – for granting me the serenity to accept the things I can not change, the courage to change the things I can, and the Wisdom to know the difference.

This book is dedicated to my mother, Shirley Allen Pratt. Words can't express how appreciative I am for all that you've done...especially letting me come back home after college so I could complete my non-paid internship with the Miami HEAT. Love always, your knucklehead.

Acknowledgements

I'm forever grateful to a host of people who made this project possible:

Lorrie-Ann "LA" Diaz, thank you to my "favorite chica" for helping me make this dream a reality. I don't know how we both found time in our busy schedules working in sports to get this done, but we did, and I'm forever grateful for your tireless contributions.

Keonna Pratt, thanks for helping your big brother see this through. From performing pre-editing before I sent it to the editor to just being a big cheerleader in my corner. You are truly appreciated!

Phil & Shannon Bynes (GoodFaithInvesting.com), Erika Swilley, Matt Meyersohn, Leslie Nixon, Esq., Tracey N. Webster, Esq., Lee Butler, Sonia Harty, Michael Lissack, David Mack, Toby Lane, Tariq Fleming, Bruce Wimbish, Kenny McCraney, the entire HEAT Group Organization and to all my family, friends and colleagues who supported me. This project would never have happened had it not been for you all.

Table of Contents

I.   Invictus...1

II.   My Story: I'm a Hustler Baby 3

III.   Why Companies Hire: Being the Solution.............................11

IV.   Pratt Triple H Theory to Success and the Golden Rule
        of Success...13

V.   Why Intern? Soaking Up the Game: Learn as Much as
        You Can 17

VI.   Knowing *Who's Who*: Studying the Team Media Guide.........19

VII.   Time Will Tell: Persistence vs. Stalking and Not
        Getting Blackballed 21

VIII.   The Heart of a Good Marketing Campaign 25

IX.   Insights from the Inside 27

X.   The Saga Continues: Sink or Swim 45

I

Invictus

Out of the night that covers me,
　　Black as the Pit from pole to pole,
I thank whatever gods may be
　　For my unconquerable soul.

In the fell clutch of circumstance
　　I have not winced nor cried aloud.
Under the bludgeonings of chance
　　My head is bloody, but unbowed.

Beyond this place of wrath and tears
　　Looms but the Horror of the shade,
And yet the menace of the years
　　Finds, and shall find, me unafraid.
It matters not how strait the gate,
　　How charged with punishments the scroll,
I am the master of my fate:
　　I am the captain of my soul.

William Ernest Henley
1849–1903

II

My Story: I'm a Hustler Baby

From my experience, there are only two ways to get a job with a sports team: either you know someone on the inside or you're kicking down the door with your credentials and experience in hand.

I didn't know anyone. So let me tell you my story of how I kicked down the door.

I'm about to give you what no one gave to me: the *Jewels of the Game*—a crash course on how to get down with a sports team. My goal is to help you reach your goal by obtaining the job of your dreams working in sports.

But first, my professional credentials and why you should be listening to me.

Since February 2006, I've worked as the **Community Affairs Coordinator for the 2006 NBA Champion Miami HEAT**. I'm one of the coordinators for all the major community events for the team domestically and internationally. I've also led the Quantified Player Appearance Tracking pilot project for the NBA– a model that was adopted league-wide and designated as "Best Practice."

I'm also a **Founding Member and Current Vice President** of the Miami Chapter of the **National Association of Black Sports Professionals**, which is one of the only national associations for professionals working in the sports industry.

And finally, I'm a member of the **Board of Directors** for **Florida Atlantic University's National Alumni Association**, where my role is Vice Chair of the Athletics Committee.

Background

I came from very humble beginnings, and I had to prove myself with everything in life. My older brothers are all bigger than me, and because of my smaller size, I had to fight constantly in my neighborhood to prove myself.

I accepted two realities very early in life:

1. **Nothing will ever be given to me.**
2. **I could never let anyone define me, my capabilities or my potential.**

During my freshman year in high school, I barely made the junior varsity football team, and embarrassingly earned the title of a benchwarmer/scrub. I played a total of maybe four plays out of the hundreds that were played in the 10 games that season. It seemed like my game uniform was cleaner after the game than it was before it—go figure.

Everyone, including my parents, felt that I was hopeless in sports, but...

The single greatest decision I ever made in my entire life was to never let anyone define me, my capabilities or my potential.

I had a defiant spirit and I sought to prove everyone wrong. Shortly after football season ended my freshman year, I became a beast in the weight room. I had this ambition and motivation that was fostered out of a sense of hopelessness and desperation. That desperation evolved into an addiction to **self-development**. I would wake up at 5:00 in the morning to work out before school. I would run to the lunch line to be the first to finish my lunch, then go to the football stadium and run up and down the bleachers for the remainder of the lunch period.

My teammates used to clown me about my daily ritual. They gave me the name *Rudy*, based on the movie in the early 90's about a young man who defied all the odds, and lived out his life dream of playing football for the Norte Dame Fighting Irish. They all said I was "too small and uncoordinated" to play sports in high school.

But the single greatest decision I ever made in my entire life was to never let anyone define me, my capabilities or my potential.

The next season, not only did I make the team and became the starting safety, I also caught six interceptions –setting the record for Piper High.

By my senior year in high school, I had become a star student athlete. I was on the varsity football team, wrestling team, captain and company commander of the JROTC program, and I was obsessed with weight lifting. At 17 years old, I weighed 160 pounds and was bench-pressing 275.

Then, unexpectedly, in one night, it was all taken away.

On October 11, 1996, during a district high school football game, I was rammed on the side of my head, hyper-extending my spinal cord. The accident severely damaged my brachia plexus nerves, which are the ones that operate my right arm. My right pectoral (chest) muscles were torn off my collarbone. To be sure, I was messed up pretty badly.

The doctors told me they had good news and bad news. The bad news was I might never again be able to move my right arm. The good news was I was supposed to be paralyzed from the neck down.

The single greatest decision I ever made in my entire life was to never let anyone define me, my capabilities or my potential.

I had to complete my senior year of high school in a neck brace and a sling. I underwent a grueling rehabilitation process to regain mobility in my right arm. I'm sure you've probably had the experience of falling asleep on your arm, and not being able to move it for about 10 seconds in the morning. Well, my paralysis lasted a little longer. It was 18 months before I was able to raise my right hand above my head.

Despite my situation, I graduated high school on time and was the first in my family to graduate college. I worked two jobs to put myself through college, where I earned dual degrees in marketing and management at Florida Atlantic University (FAU). It took me a little over six years to get my degrees, but during that time I became very involved on campus, which gave me my event production, marketing and management experience.

I started out as the Advertising Chair of the Student Government Program Board: the primary event planning organization on campus, producing step shows, concerts, lectures, field trips and more. I later became the Marketing Director for the Homecoming Department, and the next year, I became the Homecoming Director.

During my last year, I was elected Student Body President and Trustee of Florida Atlantic University. As Student Body President, I was the managing director of a $5.8 million budget, and the official spokesperson of 26,000 students. I was only the fifth African-American student in the history of the university to earn that title. I was also elected Vice Chair for the Florida Student Association—the second highest Student Government Association President in the state of Florida.

I can't help but laugh when I think back to my collegiate accomplishments, and how the Miami HEAT was so *not* impressed; or at least that's what they led me to believe.

The next phase of my life I called the "rites of passage" to becoming a go-getter. I always knew I wanted to work in sports, but didn't know where to start. A friend suggested that I read Drew Rosenhaus' book, *A Shark Never Sleeps,* to learn how he broke into the industry. In doing so, I learned how Drew wanted to be a sports agent more than anything. He walked into a sports agent's office when he was a college student, and told him he would work for free just to get a chance to learn about the industry from the inside.

I was motivated by Drew's story, and set out to follow my dream. I conducted research and sought out the Director of Event Services for the Miami HEAT/AmericanAirlines Arena. I typed a letter stating, in short, "my dream and passion is to work in the sports industry and I would work for free just to gain the opportunity to learn the ropes." I enclosed my résumé (which I thought was impressive), along with the letter I sent to the HEAT offices. I sent the package via FedEx because I figured, "This is the Miami HEAT. Hundreds of college students are probably doing the same thing. I have to do something that will stand out; that will let them know I'm special." That was my justification for paying $10.00 to send a package when a mere 42 cents would have accomplished the same goal.

After I confirmed that the letter was received, I followed up by phone. On the third attempt, I was able to reach my contact. I expressed to him that I wanted to help him and his department any way I could, and would even be willing to volunteer for any event the HEAT was hosting. The Director of Event Services advised me that there was a non-paid internship opening in his department. I immediately expressed my interest and scheduled a face-to-face interview the following week.

I arrived for the interview almost an hour early. I didn't want to run the risk of being delayed by traffic. While I waited in the lobby, I became acquainted with the receptionist, whom I later learned was actually the head of Administrative Services, Sybil Wilson (she was relieving her receptionist for an afternoon break). In that moment, I was grateful to have followed my mom's advice of being courteous and respectful to all people—regardless of their position. It served me quite well that day.

Ms. Wilson and I had an interesting exchange. "Granny"—as she is affectionately known—complimented my attire, and said it seemed I was ready for business. She then gave me some very candid and valuable advice – that working in sports is not all glamour and more often than not, you really will have to put in long hours.

It makes perfect sense now. That was probably the truest and definitely the most insightful advice about working in sports. And I felt I was ready to make that personal sacrifice to achieve my goal.

The Director of Event Services, Jarred Diamond, walked into the lobby to introduce himself and take me to his office to conduct the interview. As we walked, he turned and said, "You know. You're doing pretty good. When I was trying to get my internship here, I had to call someone 15 times before I got a returned call." I chuckled to myself and thought, "That's you, not me!"

We sat down for the interview and I didn't waste any time expressing my passion for breaking into this industry. I expressed that I would do whatever it took to prove myself and that all I needed was a shot. This reminded me of my high school football days when I used to be on the sidelines jumping up and down, asking the coach to "put me in!" I didn't just feel like I was ready – I knew I was ready! All I needed was a chance.

Mr. Diamond laughed at my energy and proceeded to introduce me to the rest of his staff. One gentleman in particular stood out: Michael Hurt. Hurt was the Events Staffing Manager and a recent hire, having interned there just three months prior. Hurt also laughed at my energy and my enthusiasm. After about 35 minutes, Mr. Diamond finally stated that he had a few more interviews to conduct and would call me at the end of the week to let me know where I stood.

The end of the week came and went. No phone call from the Director of Event Services. Four weeks came and went and still no phone call. During that timeframe, I called him 17 times, left nine messages and sent two emails; all this in addition to the standard follow up *Thank You* cards I sent to every single person I met that day- including Granny, the Senior Director of Administrative Services who was dubbing as the receptionist.

I became a little discouraged and started to lose faith in the idea that the HEAT would call me. At that time I was interning for the Sports Marketing Department of my university, but my heart was with the HEAT.

One day after class, I was speaking to my favorite marketing professor about my plans after graduation. I told her of my dream to work in sports, in particular for the Miami HEAT, and how I interviewed nearly four weeks prior and heard nothing since the interview. Then something happened to revive my faith. She informed me that there was a career fair taking place the next day at the Miami HEAT offices.

Ecstatic about what I had just learned, I rushed to the computer lab and stayed up all night to complete homework and class work for the following day. I emailed my assignments to my professors with a note saying, "I'm heading to Miami tomorrow to get my internship with the Miami HEAT." The next morning, I jumped in my car and drove 50 miles from Boca Raton to downtown Miami to the HEAT offices.

Take 2

When I arrived at the career fair, I really didn't know what to expect. On the main concourse of the arena there were dozens of companies accepting résumés. I remember the HEAT table had over 100 people waiting in line to hand their résumés to the human resources recruiter, with the hopes of having the résumé put in the "priority/potential" pile.

So, I took a chance and left the career fair, walking all the way around to the other side of the building where the HEAT offices were. I greeted the receptionist very politely and said, "Afternoon ma'am. My name is Ancel Pratt. I interviewed with Mr. Diamond about four weeks ago. I drove from Boca Raton today for the career fair but was hoping I could have five minutes of his time, if he's available." I truly believe that one of the reasons the receptionist went above and beyond to try to reach Mr. Diamond was because of my politeness to her.

She called Mr. Diamond several times to no avail. She then asked if there was anyone else I could speak to, and I remembered Mike Hurt, the Events Staffing Manager who I met the day of my interview.

The receptionist got Mike Hurt on the phone on the first try and handed me the receiver. "Good day, Mr. Hurt. Hope all is well. I'm not sure if you remember me, but I met you about four weeks ago when I interviewed with Mr. Diamond for the internship. I was down from Boca Raton for the career fair and was hoping I could have a moment of your time and Mr. Diamond's time to show you how I can be an asset to your organization."

Mike Hurt started to laugh and then he put me on hold. I stood at the receptionist desk for about three minutes with the receiver to my ear. After three minutes of waiting—the receiver still in my ear—Mike Hurt then appeared from the doorway at the top of the stairwell and motioned for me to join him.

We walked into Mr. Diamond's office, where "the hardest man to catch up with" was waiting. He asked me to take a seat. Then Mr. Diamond began to explain how "after further evaluation, I've realized that there really wasn't much of a demand for our department to take on a full-time intern." For a moment, I was crushed. "But you know what?" he continued. "Out of all the people I interviewed nationwide, you're the only one that called more than twice. What people don't realize is that in this industry the squeakiest wheel gets the grease. And for that, we would like to offer you a part-time position as an usher/ticket taker supervisor. Now, this is a part-time position and doesn't pay much."

"I would do it for free!" I interrupted. "I JUST WANT TO BE A PART OF THE HEAT FAMILY!"

Fast Forward

Three weeks and 15 events into the internship, I'd already made a name for myself. **I was always the first to arrive and the last to leave the office.** I was constantly in my managers' faces asking to take on additional responsibilities.

After a meeting one day, Mr. Diamond asked me if I could come in early the following day to work on a project, which I did. When I arrived, Mr. Diamond invited me into his office. Then he confessed the following: "You know, me and my staff have been talking, and we really appreciate you always offering to help. You just won't go away, and that's a good thing. So we decided to offer you the Event Services internship." I was ecstatic.

While serving as an intern, I made it my mission to shine in everything I did. I learned to handle my primary responsibilities first and foremost, and secondly, made sure I was very liberal with offering my support to any of the managers. I studied the team media guide, which contained biographies of team executives and photos of all the employees. I have to be honest-I didn't know the names of many of the HEAT players when I was interning, but I knew all the executives by name and title. Naturally, this came in handy when I was working an event and encountered the senior managers—a prime opportunity for you to "step your game up."

My internship was discontinued after five months because I graduated from FAU, but I remained involved with The HEAT Group as a part-time supervisor for ushers/ticket takers. It was an extremely humbling time. I began doing freelance marketing and public relations work during the day, and working the concerts, events and games in the evenings.

I call this part of my life the "starving" phase. I lived on Ramen Noodles and grilled cheese sandwiches for three months—literally! I would average about $200.00 every two weeks with my freelance work, and another $100.00 or so with working as an usher/ticket taker at the arena. I had to move back home for a year while I "paid my dues" to work in sports. However, while working at the HEAT, I used my time wisely. I volunteered for every opportunity that arose, and carried myself as if I was already a full-time manager. I was personable with everyone, but made sure I presented myself in a manner that demanded respect.

Throughout the course of my five month internship, I made my name known with different managers in the organization, for being the one who always stepped up to volunteer at every opportunity. I particularly remembered volunteering at two very big Community Affairs events, where I was introduced to the Director of the department, Steve Stowe. After volunteering at one of his events, Steve sent an email to the head of the department I was interning in, expressing his appreciation for my diligence and hard work. Months later, when there was a vacancy in the Community Affairs Department, I applied, interviewed, was and hired for the position.

Let me make something perfectly clear: My marketing and business skills, event production, project management and sales experience are what qualified me to do the job. Being liked by the hiring director, volunteering, going the extra mile, being a problem solver and demonstrating with action how badly I wanted to work for the HEAT, I believe, was the deciding factor on why I was offered the position. To be qualified and have the experience is only one layer of the cake. If one cannot mesh well within an organization, then there is no icing to put on the cake. And what's cake without the icing?

III

Why Companies Hire: Being the Solution

I have spoken to thousands of high school and college students throughout the years through many speaking engagements, and I always try to drive home the simple answer to the very important question of why companies hire:

Companies hire because they have a problem and they are looking for a solution.

Now, the more important question is: "Can you be the solution to their problem?"

Think about this concept for a second. If a grocery store is hiring cashiers, one could interpret the problem as being an insufficient number of employees available to help customers get through the grocery line quickly and efficiently.

Similarly, if a retail store is hiring to fill the position of overnight stock clerk, perhaps the problem is that the company has their products delivered late at night, after store hours, and they need help with getting the shelves stocked and the store ready for the next business day.

Companies have vacancies (i.e., a problem). You need a job (i.e., a solution). If a company hires you, it's likely you have a skill set they need and want. And more often than not, their decision to hire you focuses on four main points: (1) you have the ability to get the work done; (2) you fit into their company culture; (3) they like you; and (4) they can afford you.

There is one more challenge you have to deal with when you are striving to get a job working in sports and that is convincing the company that you are not just "a solution" to their problems, but that you are the *best* solution. Let's imagine there is a vacancy in the community affairs department, where you could potentially have over 100 people apply for a single job. I'm confident in saying that out of those 100 applicants, we should be able to find at least 20 that are qualified to do the job. But it shouldn't be your goal to be deemed *qualified*, but to actually be considered the *best* choice and get the job.

Having said this, it's up to you, then, to show them what you've got.

IV

Pratt Triple H Theory to Success and the Golden Rule of Success

There are three H's upon which I've built my success.

The first H stands for **HUMBLE**. Whether you like it or not, this game will humble you. I recommend that you *willingly humble yourself to a person or process that can help you reach your goals.*

When explaining this concept, I always like to reference the popular hit TV series "Making the Band" starring Sean "P. Diddy" Combs. In the second season of the show, Combs moved the first band into his house, and granted them access to his studio, resources, network and mentorship—all in an effort to help them realize their dream of making it in the music industry.

One night, while at a studio session, Combs stops the session and tells the band that he's hungry and has a craving for a cheesecake. He asks the band members to walk across town to get him cheesecake. They walk out of the studio and begin debating Combs' request. Five minutes into the debate, Combs goes outside and is dismayed the band hasn't yet left.

He erupts: "WTF? Why haven't you left yet?" One of the band members responds, "We think you are just trying to play us by sending us way across town to get you a cheesecake. We don't see what this has got to do with why we are here."

Combs confided, "Let me let you in on a little secret. In this industry and in this profession, you always have to do something you don't want to do. I opened up my house and my studio to you and not for me but to help *you* realize your goals. So, if you can do this without me, get your sh*t out of my house and do what you got to do! Otherwise, go get my god damned cheesecake and be happy about it!"

Moral of the story, **we all have to pay our dues**—including you!

The second H stands for **HUNGER**. Remember what Jarred Diamond told me: "In this industry, the squeakiest wheel gets the grease." I didn't have the highest GPA out of all the applicants, and I certainly didn't know anyone that worked at the Miami HEAT. The single most important reason why I got the job over everyone else is because **no one else wanted it more badly than I did!** And I proved it.

My whole life has been a series of experiences paying dues; going above and beyond to prove myself. It seemed just natural that proving myself was something I had to do. But what's amazing to me is the number of people I've spoken to during my tenure with the HEAT who believe everything should be given to them.

There is a quote by Henry Wadsworth Longfellow I learned in college that so eloquently conveys this principle:

"The heights by great men reached and kept were not obtained by sudden flight, but they, while their companions slept, were toiling upward through the night."

The first line highlights that it's not enough to merely reach the top—you have to *stay* at the top. A boxer who works all his life trying to be a heavyweight champion isn't really satisfied with just becoming the champ. He wants to remain a champion as long as he can. Also, reaching the top is not going to happen overnight. To be frank, there is no such thing as an overnight success, except for lottery winners and well, you know the odds of winning the lottery!

When I was hired full-time as the Community Affairs Assistant, there wasn't a day that went by where I didn't have to "prove myself." It was like the movie *The Devil Wears Prada*, where everyone kept telling the main character: "A million people would kill to have your job!" This scenario became my reality.

I remember five weeks into the job I made a mistake on a project. In the three weeks that followed, my director forwarded to me a series of voicemails by college students and recent graduates. Those voicemails expressed how they would do whatever it took to work for him. At first, I thought, "WTF?" But then it hit me: like the boxing champ, everyone is coming for his crown. **Now that I have the job, I have to stay hungry if I want to keep it!**

The last line of Longfellow's quote emphasizes that success is obtained by those who go the extra mile. In sports, there is a saying, "Championships are won in the off season." Victory usually goes to those who are better prepared—which means while your competition is resting, you should be working.

The last H stands for **HAVE A GAME PLAN.** Far too often people are ill-prepared. They delve into a project or a job without a solid game plan. Not having a game plan is one of the quickest and surest ways to fail.

HUMBLE. HUNGER. HAVE A GAME PLAN.

These three principles are supported by what I call the Golden Rule of Success: **DON'T QUIT!**

When things go wrong, and they sometimes will
When the road you're trotting seems all uphill
When the funds are low and the debt is high
When you want to smile but have to sigh

When care is pressing you down a bit
Rest you must, but DON'T QUIT!!

Success is failure turned inside out
The silver line in the cloud of doubt
And you never know how close you are
It may be near when it seems afar

So stick to the fight when you're hardest hit
Because it's at that time, YOU MUSTN'T QUIT!

- Anonymous

V

Why Intern?
Soaking Up the Game: Learn as Much as You Can

Robert Kiyosaki, author of *Rich Dad, Poor Dad* said it best: "The rich don't work for money, they work to learn." And so should you!

Many college graduates complain they can't find jobs because prospective employers want applicants to have some experience. But how can you gain experience if no one will give you a job? It's the classic example of a catch-22. But the answer is quite simple: **interning**. An internship is the way you get hands-on experience.

As an intern, your primary responsibility is to gather information and garner experience. Your goal is to act like a sponge and soak up knowledge and expertise from industry leaders, as well as garner practical hands-on experience from your daily work. This is a *quid pro quo* relationship; they're getting a low cost worker, and you're gaining invaluable tutorship and experience in the industry.

An internship is a lot like test driving a car—for both parties. From the employer's perspective, an internship allows the employer to gauge your interest and abilities. Likewise, as an intern, you have the opportunity to gauge your prospective employer, the working environment, corporate culture and fellow employees.

Assuming the internship is the right fit and the partnership is successful, I recommend you develop your skills and confidence, so once an employer tests what you have to offer, the decision to hire you is clear.

As one of my mentors once put it, "Everybody talks a good game but I want to see you back it up. Telling me you are the best for the job is like telling me you can bake the best cake. Don't tell me you can bake a good cake; give me a slice."

VI

Knowing *Who's Who*: Studying the Team Media Guide

When I interviewed with the Miami HEAT, it was the Senior Director of Administrative Services who was manning the phones while the receptionist took a lunch break. Lucky for me, I am polite and courteous with everyone I meet.

But let's just imagine for a moment what would've happened if I would've been condescending towards her? This person, I later learned, is one of the *original* HEAT employees, and has worked for the organization for over 20 years. Suffice it to say, she likely has some say in the company's hiring practices. Any impoliteness or rudeness on my part could have adversely affected my chances of landing a job.

This is a key reason why it's a good idea to know the *Who's Who* of a potential employer. Everyone is flattered when someone knows something about them that is not obvious. This shows that you did your homework, and usually is interpreted as "you really want this." It also allows you to build on similarities that may exist between the two of you (e.g., being from the same city or graduates of the same college). In my brief exchange with the head of Administrative Services while waiting to be interviewed, I learned that she was of Caribbean decent, similar to me. It's always a plus whenever you're able to draw a positive association between you and a potential employer.

So how do you learn about your prospective employer?

Every team in professional sports creates an annual media guide, containing the entire history of the franchise, statistical information, player information, biographies of team personnel, executives, etc. If you cannot afford to purchase a media guide (usually available for sale at the team's retail store or on their website), I recommend you conduct your research on the team's website. Study the information.

Familiarize yourself with the organization, its culture and history. Know your prospective employer inside and out.

My Wizard of Oz Theory

In the popular 1939 musical *The Wizard of Oz*, the title character, we are led to believe, is an "all powerful, all knowing" demigod to be feared. But by the end of the movie, he is exposed as a regular person with the same insecurities and limitations as all the other characters in the movie.

Similarly, managers, directors and executives all have one thing in common: they are all human. They all get stressed; they all have bad days; they all have likes and dislikes just as anyone else does.

The reason I bring this up is for you to understand that no one knows what subjective cues may make you stand out favorably or unfavorably, so I recommend that you focus all your time and energy on the objective qualities that you have direct control over (e.g. professionalism, punctuality, knowledge of the company, responsibilities of the position you're applying for, etc.). You would be amazed at how many people psyche themselves out of the game and give up before even trying. I believe Wayne Gretzky said it best:

"You will miss 100% of the shots you don't take."

Don't worry about the things you cannot control, but instead strengthen your position on the things you can control.

"Life is 10% what happens to you and 90% how you react to it."
– Charles R. Swindoll

VII

Time Will Tell: Persistence vs. Stalking and Not Getting Blackballed

Nine times out of 10, an intern will hope he/she gets offered a job well before the job is even offered. Many individuals have interned with a sports team for over a year before they are offered a full time position. Don't even think about complaining about any aspect of your internship—especially not after two or three months.

Timing is everything! Be persistent. Success is the intersection between preparation and opportunity. At times, you can put yourself in a better position to take advantage of different opportunities, and others, you just have to do your best to ride it out. It is at this time when you really have to evaluate how badly you want it.

For those who don't know, there is a difference between persistence and having "stalker tendencies." The tone of your approach makes all the difference between impressing versus annoying a potential employer. Don't do anything to hurt your chances, or worse, get blackballed.

Be succinct and to the point whenever reaching out to anyone. Above all, **know why you are calling your contact.** Nothing is more irritating when people call a potential employer and don't know what they want. I tell college students, "people contact me at the HEAT office usually for one of two things: either for something I can do for them, or something I can't. All I want to know in the first 20 seconds is which one it is." There's no sense in wasting each other's time. This is especially true when you're reaching out to a senior manager or executive. Rest assured that executive got his or her position by being organized and efficient with his/her time. The last thing he/she wants to do is spend time on the phone with you while you try to figure out why you are calling.

One helpful hint is to write out what you want to say to the person before you pick up the phone. A script will help you remain focused.

<u>Making the Call</u>

Here's my recommendation for making the call (proposed script):

> *Caller:* Good morning/afternoon Ms. Diaz. My name is Peter Gabe. I got your contact information from the Miami HEAT website. Did I catch you at a bad time?

> *Ms. Diaz:* No, I have a moment. How can I help you?

> *Caller:* I was calling because it has always been my dream to work in sports, and I understand that it is a very competitive industry to break into. You work for the Miami HEAT, which means you are the best of the best at what you do. It would be an honor to learn from the best in the industry. To make sure I'm bringing to the table what you're looking for in an apprentice, would you mind telling me what skills stand out more to you in an intern?

This question is key! It allows you to get feedback directly from the decision maker on what you could do to increase your chances of getting the internship. It also allows you the opportunity to stand out. Flattery never hurts, as long as it's sincere. You didn't make the mistake that hundreds of people make by calling someone with only your agenda in mind. Remember why companies hire: they have a problem, and they need a solution. Your purpose for calling is to introduce yourself to the company and convey to that decision maker what you can do for the organization, not what the organization can do for you.

Here's my recommendation for making the call if your prospect is busy (proposed script):

> *Caller:* Good morning/afternoon Ms. Diaz. My name is Peter Gabe. I got your contact information from the Miami HEAT website. Did I catch you at a bad time?

> *Ms. Diaz:* Actually, I'm in the middle of something.

> *Caller:* I understand. I was calling to ask you a few questions about the internship. When would be a good time to follow up with you, Ms. Diaz?

This tells your prospect you are sensitive to his/her schedule, but it also reiterates your interest, because you've asked your prospect to pinpoint a specific and more convenient time for follow up.

Before you make the call, always know what you want to ask, and have a pen and paper in hand. The people you are calling are important and busy. Their time is very valuable.

For example, if you called me, and I offered you information and you were not prepared (e.g., you asked me to hold while you get a pen and pad), I would hang the phone up on you because what you unconsciously communicated to me is that:

1. You're not confident in your ability to get through to or reach someone who would give you what you want. So, if you're not confident in yourself, why should I be confident in you?

2. You're not prepared. So, if you are not prepared to take down information that could benefit you, why should I believe you would be prepared to handle any assignment I can potentially give you?

3. You don't respect me or my time. Time is the most precious commodity for the simple fact that you can't get it back. As you may have already experienced, sports professionals don't call people back that often, mainly the result of severe time constraints. If you *do* manage to get someone on the phone, make sure you are courteous of his/her time.

Keep in mind this is not to say that every sports professional you contact will be short with you on the phone but it's probably best to be prepared in case it does happen.

"Success is when preparation meets opportunity." – Henry Hartman

VIII

The Heart of a Good Marketing Campaign

Make no mistake, job hunting is a sales activity, and an interview is like a sales pitch. You're pitching the company on why it should buy your product: You. But make sure your product can live up to its advertising.

In college, I was taught that "The heart of a good marketing campaign is a great product."

Because of the high demand for sports industry jobs, you not only have to be good at what you do, you have to be great! Going back to "Why companies hire" you must first and foremost have the technical skills to be able to solve the problem they have. No matter how bad you want it, or how much you feel you will go the extra mile to prove it, if you don't have the necessary skills (accounting, bookkeeping, marketing, copywriting, etc.) to help the company address the problem they have, your go-getter efforts really won't hold much weight. Just because someone is truly passionate about working in sports doesn't mean that they are qualified to work in sports.

Develop your skills first and foremost, and then focus the extra energy in promoting yourself to the team. A great marketing campaign for an inferior product can expedite the demise of that product.

IX

Insights from the Inside

The following Q&A was crafted to offer you invaluable words of wisdom from other executives who work in professional sports.

Please note that all of the interviews were given after the chapters were completed and none of the interviewees had knowledge of what each other said or what was written in the book, prior to conducting their interview.

Sonia Harty
Vice President, Human Resources
The HEAT Group

How did you get your start working in sports?

It was purely coincidental. Human Resources is for the most part the same no matter the industry. I had experience in Human Resources when I worked for an electronic security company. A head hunter had my résumé and contacted me. Initially, I had no idea I was applying for a sports team.

What's the greatest advice you could give someone trying to break into the sports industry?

Especially for those looking to get into sports marketing and sales, an internship is key! Whatever experience you can get prior to graduation is beneficial. If I have two applicants fresh out of college, one of them has multiple internships and the other doesn't, I'm going to go with the one with the most experience every time. Networking and building contacts is also important.

What do potential candidates for employment/internships do to hurt their chances of getting into sports?

Not having a résumé that's sharp. And by sharp I mean free of grammatical errors and that's formatted appropriately. We receive hundreds of résumés where the font is either too difficult to read or the formatting is bad. Guess what? We don't even bother to look at those.

We need to get a feel for you at a glance. We're trying to quicken the process and just one mistake may be the deciding factor on whether we go with you or someone else.

One of my biggest professional pet peeves is when someone thinks that because he/she is a sports fan, that makes him/her a viable candidate to work in sports. You have to balance showing your love for a sport with your eagerness to work for a company.

Erika Swilley
Assistant Director, Community Affairs
Detroit Pistons & Detroit Shock

How did you get your start working in sports?

I got my start working in sports after submitting my résumé for an open position in the Community Relations Department I saw online. I had worked many internships and jobs in the entertainment industry, but knew I wanted to get into sports, so I started to search for jobs in the field. While I never interned or worked for a sports organization prior to me landing my current job, I made sure to take positions that would give me the experience needed to make the transition.

What's the greatest advice you could give someone trying to break into the sports industry?

The best advice I could give someone trying to break into the sports industry is to intern with a company in the industry or one that is comparable. Sports is a very fast-paced environment and not for everyone. A lot of people have a skewed idea of what working in sports is going to be like, and it is important that they have realistic expectations before trying to make it their career. Also, it is not about "*who* you know," but "*who knows you.*" Make an impression on everyone you meet. You never know when someone will be able to help you later on.

What do potential candidates for employment/internships do to hurt their chances of getting into sports?

Mistakes that potential candidates for employment/internships in sports commonly make is thinking being a huge sports fan will get them the job. Great that you are a fan, but if you don't know the business side of things, you will never succeed. It is a major turnoff when in an interview a candidate mentions being excited about meeting a player, or doesn't know our programming. We want you to know our players, but we are not looking to hire fans.

Matt Meyersohn
Manager, Community Affairs
Boston Celtics

How did you get your start working in sports?

I got my start in sports by working an internship while in college. A friend of mine did an internship with the Celtics, and he worked full-time, so I applied for a fulltime non-paid internship, living out of my parents' basement. I did a full season of internship, and worked part-time to make ends meet.

I got hired for the NBA working in the Events and Attractions group on a tour called "Rhythm and Rims." I spent five months in Denver working at the NBA satellite office for the NBA All-Star Jam session. Then I went on tour again the following summer and returned home to work for the New England Patriots for a little over one year, starting in events and moving over to the Community Affairs Department.

It took almost three years for the Celtics to have an opening in the Community Affairs Department, but when they did, they remembered me, and I got the call to interview for the position.

What's the greatest advice you could give someone trying to break into the sports industry?

If possible, start doing internships while in college or even in high school.

What do potential candidates for employment/internships do to hurt their chances of getting into sports?

Not editing their résumé or cover letter. Any mistakes let me know you don't want it bad enough. Also, being too much of a fan, and not having an understanding of what the work requires.

Lastly, my **biggest pet peeve** is when someone is unprepared for the interview. You should easily spend a few hours on our website researching the company and programs that we do. If I ask you "which program of ours do you like the most" and you give me an answer like "the one where you work with the community," I thank you for wasting your time and mine and the interview is over.

It never made sense to me how college students would study hours and put in more time for a test than they would for a job interview. It's crazy!

Leslie Nixon, Esquire
Manager of Volunteer Programs
The Miami Dolphins

How did you get your start working in sports?

I was fortunate enough to meet my first boss when he was guest lecturing in a class for my Sport Administration Masters program. I was able to successfully network my way into my first job in sports. So remember to always make a great first impression and network.

What's the greatest advice you could give someone trying to break into the sports industry?

Volunteer and network. Volunteering can help build your sports résumé and help you to discern the area in sports in which you would like to work. Believe it or not, employers can tell whether or not you would be interested in doing the job during the interview.

Employers are not going to hire a person if they are not interested in the job, even if they are qualified. Also, employers do not want to be your personal career laboratory. They want to find people who can start immediately making an impact in the company, rather than someone who is just looking to sample the opportunity.

Volunteering and networking will help you to get to know the professionals in your region. When you get to know the players in the field and they get to know you, there are certain perks that come about. For instance, many sports professionals email their networks of job opportunities open within their company. Sometimes, they might even recommend you for a position. Just remember that the more people you know and the more people that know you can drastically increase your chances of getting a job in sports.

What do potential candidates for employment/internships do to hurt their chances of getting into sports?

The best suggestion that I can provide any person looking for a job in sports is to refrain from saying in the interview that you are a huge fan of sports, that you love watching sports, etc. When working in sports, you very rarely get the opportunity to sit back and enjoy the actual sporting events.

What this says to the interviewer is that you don't truly know what it means to work in sports, and that you would be an awesome season ticket holder, not employee. So first, learn what it means to work in sports, and then what it means to successfully do the work required of the potential job. Convey this to the interviewer while you highlight why you would be the perfect fit.

Lee Butler
Associate Director, Championships
Atlantic Coast Conference (ACC)

How did you get your start working in sports?

I got my start in sports by working with the women's basketball team at the University of Miami (UM). From 2003-2004, I assisted the Head Women's Basketball Manager with video responsibilities and served as a male practice player after being told that the men's team would not accept additional walk-ons. With the exception of working summer basketball camps at George Mason University, this was my first paying job in athletics. In the fall of 2004, I walked-on to the men's basketball team and played two years for coach Frank Haith. This led to my next opportunity in sports. Upon graduation, I was awarded an ACC Futures Internship (internship program for graduating student athletes) at the ACC Office in Greensboro, NC. This was my introduction into the administration of college athletics.

What's the greatest advice you could give someone trying to break into the sports industry?

My advice to someone trying to break into the industry is to number one, find out if sports is really your passion. Volunteer or intern at local sporting events to see if the long hours and minimal monetary compensation bothers you. Nearly as important is building your professional network. People only hire people they can trust. And initially that employer's trust is going to come from a recommendation someone makes on your behalf. A good network will also aid in identifying good organizations that fit a candidate's strengths. And the third piece of advice is something a college professor once told me: "no job is too small." Whatever task you are assigned, embrace it and do it better than everybody else.

What do potential candidates for employment/internships do to hurt their chances of getting into sports?

Candidates hurt their chances by looking to step right into their dream job. Before you can become that GM, Head Coach, or Athletics Director, you have to build a foundation. And that foundation is likely going to be built with entry level responsibility, long hours, and little money. Being ambitious is great but being realistic is more important. Take that $20,000 job, do it better than anyone before you, and let your work propel you up the corporate ladder!

Michael Lissack,
Assistant Director, Sports Media Relations
The Miami HEAT

How did you get your start working in sports?

I got my start in sports when I was the photography editor of my high school newspaper. We were doing a story on a 76ers player and I called up their PR department to see if I could take some photos during a game.

From that point on, I kept in contact with the PR director of the 76ers, which eventually led her to help me get a summer internship with the head statistician of the 76ers. The head statistician turned out to be a gentleman named Harvey Pollack, who has been involved in the NBA since its inception, and is well known throughout the league. After that summer internship, he called the Boston Celtics (I went to school in Boston), to see if I could help them out during the season. That led to me helping out at games during my sophomore year.

From that point on, it went back and forth. The summer after I went back and worked with Harvey. Then during my junior year, I did an internship with the Celtics PR department. The following summer, I went back to the 76ers, but this time did an internship with their PR department. My senior year was the NBA lockout, so I did a game-night internship with the Boston Bruins of the NHL, and worked in Boston University's Sports Marketing Department. When the lockout ended during my second semester, I continued to work with the Bruins, but also went back and worked with the Celtics. The following summer, I was back at the 76ers PR department until I got a full time job.

The reason why I believe internships are so important is because I got my first full time job with the Golden State Warriors through the urging of the former 76ers PR director, who originally gave me my start in sports. I went back and worked full time for the Celtics from 2000-2004 because a position opened up and they knew and liked me from when I was an intern. Finally, I moved to Miami and am about to start my sixth full season here. My boss here was my former boss at the 76ers, for whom I interned.

What's the greatest advice you could give someone trying to break into the sports industry?

Obviously, from what I wrote above, the best advice I can give is to do an internship. Teams like to hire from within and hire people who they know and have seen in a working environment. The Sports Industry is a tough field to get into, and you can't automatically jump into the highest level. If you are in school, see if you can work with the school's athletic department. There are also minor league teams you could work for if your city does not have a professional team. Don't assume that just because you want to work in professional sports, that working for a school or minor league won't provide you with valuable experience that will look good on a résumé.

What do potential candidates for employment/internships do to hurt their chances of getting into sports?

The biggest mistake I have seen people make is the misconception about what working in professional sports is all about. Most fans just see the glamorous side, but it is not always like that. In my position, from October through (hopefully) June, I work almost seven days a week, at night, on weekends, during holidays. My schedule and free time is based solely on the team and I have no control over it. A typical game day is a 16 hour day, and when I travel with the team, there are times when you arrive back in Miami at 2:00 or 3:00 a.m. and have to be in the office at 9:00 a.m.

Also, it is important to realize that becoming friendly with the athletes is not what the job is about. You need to remain a professional and understand that the life you lead varies greatly from theirs. The job certainly has its perks, but it is not all glamour.

Dave Mack
Group Sales Account Manager
The Miami HEAT

How did you get your start in sports?

I volunteered for various sports-related events throughout college. I joined the Sport Management Society, majored in Sport Management and minored in Business, and maintained a sports-related summer job all four years in college. Then I landed a 10-month internship with the Orlando Magic after attending an NBA job fair in Orlando, Florida – three months prior to graduating. The internship was paid, but it was only a $300.00 stipend every two weeks. We worked an average of six days a week and I once worked 13 days straight! I also had to dress up as a Magic Dancer, got sling-shotted across the court into trash cans as a human bowling ball, chugged a 12-ounce glass of gravy on Thanksgiving and even wore the mascot's costume on several occasions to fill in. After the 10-month internship, I was hired full-time.

What's the greatest advice you could give someone trying to break into the sports industry?

Talk to as many people as you can and never underestimate anyone! You never know who you are going to meet, so increase your odds of success by participating and volunteering for as much as you can. And the most important thing – follow up with your contacts.

What do potential candidates for employment/internships do to hurt their chances of getting into sports?

Job candidates hurt their chances for employment/internships by not believing in themselves. If you really want to work in pro sports one day, you will. With all of the professional, semi-professional and collegiate teams out there, it is impossible to get turned away from every team. Once you get your foot in the door, be the best you can be and make a great first impression. Also, if you call a certain team and they are not hiring at the moment, be persistent and follow up with that organization. Failure to follow up and failure to ask about job openings will give you a 0% chance of landing that job.

Toby Lane
Associate Director of Basketball Operations
University of Miami (FL)

How did you get your start in sports?

I grew up playing sports, and that was my favorite thing to do. Since I was six years old, all I wanted to do was play sports or be in sports. In college, I played for two years at Mid-America Bible College in Oklahoma City (a small, non-scholarship school), then transferred to the larger Wichita State University, where I obtained a math education degree. I wanted to be a teacher so I could also coach. I taught math and coached a boys' basketball team at a small, 1A high school in Kansas. After teaching and coaching high school, I worked at Neosho County Community College, University of Central Oklahoma (as graduate assistant and full-time assistant), Long Beach State, University of Oklahoma, Southeast Missouri State University, and now the University of Miami (FL).

What's the greatest advice you could give someone trying to break into the sports industry?

Those who want a career in sports should work hard, follow their passion, and get involved (working or volunteering) as soon as possible in life, preferably in college. I worked for Coach Kelvin Sampson at the University of Oklahoma and he always said, "If you work hard you aren't guaranteed to succeed, but if you don't work hard, you are guaranteed to fail." Possessing a very strong work ethic allows one to get through obstacles and find a way to "get it done." With a very strong work ethic that is part of who you are, those who can help you advance in your career will take notice and start putting their trust in you. Leaders and supervisors will promote those who work hard, who obviously have the needed skills, more so than those who do not work hard.

Following your passion makes it possible to show that exceptional work ethic that pushes you above and beyond others. It is very difficult to achieve at high levels unless you have a passion that helps to fight through obstacles. When you love what you do, it doesn't feel like work.

Getting involved in your passion and area of concentration as early as possible helps with developing your skills and contacts. Working sports camps, coaching youth or AAU teams, working with high schools, colleges, or professional teams, or volunteering for sports organizations (YMCA, instructional academies, camps) are great ways to get the experience and contacts to push you ahead.

I really don't have many regrets in my life, but one of my regrets is not being a basketball manager during the last three years of my undergraduate college career. It would have taken me one more year to graduate from college, but it would have greatly contributed to my development as a person and coach, and started me on a great road of developing contacts in college basketball. It would have been a sacrifice, but I really believe it would have paid off in the future.

What do potential candidates for employment/internships do to hurt their chances of getting into sports?

Those who don't work hard do not help themselves in their career, even killing chances of developing their career. Supervisors and leaders hate it when those they lead aren't willing to work hard and find excuses to not work. If you want to get ahead and achieve at a high level, you must work hard and have a strong work ethic. I don't like working with people who don't work hard, and won't recommend people who don't work hard.

Tariq W. Fleming
Account Executive, Season Ticket Sales
Bobcats Sports & Entertainment

How did you get your start in sports?

I have been involved in sports my entire life. My first sports job was as an umpire in the baseball league I grew up in – in my neighborhood on south side Chicago. Through that job, I babysat for a family for over five years. The father, Ian Mahoney, ended up getting a job as Director of Administration for the New York Knicks with Ed Tapscott, the Assistant General Manager then. As soon as Ian took the position, his first call was to me. Being well aware of my aspirations to work in sports, he invited me to come out and intern for the team in Basketball Operations. That, ironically, is how I got my first position in pro sports – small world.

What's the greatest advice you could give someone trying to break into the sports industry?

As far as the advice I would give to a young man or woman out there trying to get a job in general, let alone pro sports – it's very simple. First thing is to make sure the résumé matches the job you desire. If you want to apply to be a sanitation worker, make sure you highlight the work you have done in the past that qualifies you as the best person applying for the job. Also, don't be afraid to try new methods to get the attention of the person making the hiring decisions. One example was when a good friend of mine sent a brand new sneaker to a coach. Inside the sneaker was a note asking how he could get his other foot in the door. While this can be a hit or miss approach, it was the creativity that led to him getting a call back for an interview. Also, following up is very important. Remember everyone's name you come across during the interview process (even the front desk secretary), and little things like that will help you stand out. Don't burn any bridges and send thank you letters to everyone, even for the smallest things. It's the little things in the HUGE job market that makes individuals standout. Energy, enthusiasm and passion for your career (and not just the job) are what stand out the most to those trying to figure out whether or not to invest in you.

What do potential candidates for employment/internships do to hurt their chances of getting into sports?

The most important thing is to relax and be yourself. Dress the part. Shine your shoes, get a fresh haircut (sorry, got to cut the braids). Look people in the eye when you shake hands and speak, and by all means FOLLOW UP. Thank you letters (even an email from your Blackberry on the way home from the interview) goes a long way. Sometimes doing small things are taken for granted and can make the difference in whether you or the next person is hired.

Bruce Wimbish
Basketball Communications Manager
Cleveland Cavaliers

How did you get your start in sports?

My story has a couple of twists and turns. The light bulb for being in the sports industry came on late for me at the University of Cincinnati. It wasn't until my senior year that I started to drift toward the sports and entertainment industry. It was 2000 and the economy was really bad, so I ended up getting my MBA immediately after I completed my undergraduate work. I didn't have a lot of experience in sports and hadn't taken any classes, so during graduate school I was not successful at applying for opportunities in professional sports/college athletics. I really struggled in those two years of getting my MBA. The last quarter of my program I did take a Sports Marketing class, and realized that Ohio State offered a Sports Management Masters program.

After taking one year off following graduation, I applied to Ohio State for their program, and was accepted. Upon acceptance I was able to start an internship with the Columbus Blue Jackets. I didn't know anything about hockey at the time, but the internship was in corporate sales. I was able to apply my MBA and business background to the position. I was with the Blue Jackets for a season and a half while at Ohio State. I also got to work on a start up with the Columbus Destroyers, which was an arena football league team that was an expansion franchise, and I did that for their first full season.

In the summer of 2004, I needed to do another internship somewhere different. That's when I came to the Cleveland Cavaliers as a marketing intern. I did that for the summer, and at the end of the term they had a position in Communications, where again my MBA and my Masters in Sports really helped. I didn't have the journalism or communications background, but they felt my business degree was great for this newly created position called Corporate Communications. And so that was my "in" into sports. I worked in Corporate Communications for four years and moved over to the basketball side in the last two seasons.

What's the greatest advice you could give someone trying to break into the sports industry?

My best advice would be to determine your interests and your passion early on. Being at the undergraduate level you don't have to necessarily do a graduate degree, at least not right away, in order to get your start in sports. But the sooner you discover your interest, the more you can focus on doing internships, volunteering, and getting that sports experience. That will make you more competitive than other candidates coming out of school and applying for jobs. The other thing about getting your early start is that it also gives you the time to try out different areas, and helps you to find out what you're interested in – whether it's sales, marketing, communications, community relations - all different diciplines. The earlier you start, the more time you get to work in different areas.

What do potential candidates for employment/internships do to hurt their chances of getting into sports?

They hurt their chances by thinking that their degree is all that they need. Sports is extremely competitive more so than people understand. In addition to education and experience, you also need to have that network: to have people pulling on your behalf and making phone calls and sending emails. Again, that goes back to trying to get as much experience as early on as possible, because the longer you have been in the field, the more time you have had to network and build those relationships. Even though sports is growing and there would be a lot of opportunities available, it is still a small world once you are working in it. The people you know – they know other people, and the world just gets a lot smaller from there.

Kenny McCraney
Director of Team Services
The Miami HEAT

How did you get your start in sports?

I played basketball in high school and I went to the University of Florida as a walk-on. When I was there I earned a scholarship. Not being a star player, part of my routine was making sure I worked really hard, had a lot of enthusiasm, always gave my best, had a smile on my face and just played hard. As I was graduating, I was offered a job by the head coach to be a full-time assistant coach, which I had no desire to do. Because of my enthusiasm, work ethic, and being a people-person, the head coach saw something in me that could transcend into being an assistant coach – someone who could help him build his program. As I got into coaching, I enjoyed it. I ended up getting some very good players for the University of Florida. We won the first SCC Championship. Some of those same attributes I talked about – working hard, smiling, being a people-person, being able to adapt and being humble – were some of the things that got us through.

I went into a junior college and had some success as a head coach. Then I went to Florida International University as a Division I coach, and did the same things in terms of getting good players and having a lot of success where people didn't have a lot of success before. The same attributes helped: humility, being happy, working hard and trying to outwork everybody else. Being consistent is what seemed to get me places.

I eventually had to move on from FIU, but an opportunity opened up at the Miami HEAT with Ronald Rastein, a friend of mine through college. I was able to intern with the HEAT. Applying those same attributes from before moved me up from video coordinator intern to coaching assistant and scout. From there I moved to Team Services and Player Development for the Miami HEAT.

What's the greatest advice you could give someone trying to break into the sports industry?

First of all, make sure this is something you really want to do. I know a lot of people who think they want to do it, but it's a lot of hard work. It's a very guarded industry. Make sure this is something you really want to do, and if you want to get in there, be willing to wait. Be willing to go in and work hard, understand it's going to take some time, understand that you are in a special place and that you're going have to pay your dues. Show people what you can do, but again it's all going to take some time. Have money saved, be on a budget, and you can make it through. Humility is great, working hard is something you should always do, and be loyal to your bosses. My dad always told me to learn everything that you can, don't complain and learn the business. Once you learn the business and know how to do a little of everything, you really help yourself.

What do potential candidates for employment/internships do to hurt their chances of getting into sports?

One: Trying to move too fast. Two: Talking too much. While interning, it is a time to be quiet unless you are asking a question. Most of the time when you get into athletics (major college and pro), you're running into a machine that has been working really well. The only thing that usually is broken is the team, so you have coaches and GMs always working on them. But the inner workings of the industry work pretty smoothly, and something you are privileged to be a part of. Be humble, be quiet, learn, be helpful, move along smoothly without making a ripple, and work your butt off until you are noticed. Do the things they need you to do, and understand there is probably a line of folks who would love to be in the situation you are in. If you take these steps, you can land yourself a job and be happy with what you're doing.

X

The Saga Continues:
Sink or Swim

When I was hired as the Community Affairs Assistant, my then-boss told me, "The best advice I can give you to prepare mentally to work in sports is imagine being tossed into the water and told to **sink or swim**." There are going to be times when you won't have the luxury of asking questions, you just have to **make it happen**. This reinforces the fact that at bare minimum, you need the technical skills to do the work, which in a high demand industry, **just enough is not good enough**. However, if you posses the qualities of a **go-getter**, hard worker and someone who can think quickly, creatively and rationally on your feet, you put yourself in a far better position than the former. Remember, companies hire because they have a problem and need a solution. There have been many times I've been asked to get something done that others see as impossible (believe me, I have my fair share of stories and triumphs). Your boss is not interested in excuses and probably doesn't care how you get the job done, as long as you get it done and to their standards.

Like me and the rest of the interviewees in this book, you're going to face your fair share of obstacles in the pursuit of obtaining your dream job in sports. The question is, **will your circumstances outweigh your goals and dreams: getting your dream job in sports**?

There are over 480 Sports Management programs across the country; each one filled with students whose dream it is to work in sports. This doesn't even take into account those who are in general business programs who also want to work in the sports industry. Let's state the obvious: there's not enough room for every single person in all the programs to get a job working in sports. However, I'm confident that if you follow the "Jewels of the Game" laid out for you in this book, you, too, will be able to add your triumph story to this saga and join the exclusive group of those who **paid their dues** to work in the sports industry.

"If you're not on the way then you're in the way." – Dr. Lee Jones

THE SAGA CONTINUES. . . What do <u>you</u> have to offer?

Made in the USA
Lexington, KY
07 April 2014